Letters from

Heavenly Father

(enlarged print)

By Hanna Sara
May 2021

Title: Letters from Heavenly Father (enlarged print)
Author: Hanna Sara
ISBN: 978-957-438987-2
First Edition: May. 2021
Email: askhannasara@gmail.com
Web: www.hannasara.com

Preface

For God so loved the world, that he gave his only begotten Son, that whoever believes in him should not perish, but have everlasting life. [John3:16] God, our Heavenly Father, is so loving us. By Jesus' finished work and resurrection, we may enjoy a wonderful life and eternal life with Heavenly Father. However, days on earth may have some challenges. This book, based on the revelation & inspiration from the Holy Bible scriptures, presents as loving letters from Heavenly Father God to us for situations that we may face on earth. May these letters of love & wisdom light up your life.

Love in Jesus,
    Hanna

My beloved child,

The regret for the past is always coming to your mind. However, remember that you are a new creation, the old things did pass away, and all became new! [2Co.5:17] Do forget those already happened and reach forth to the glory ahead. [Phl.3:13] Because I have a plan to prosper you [Jer.29:11], and because I love you. [Rev.3:9]

    Heavenly Father who deeply loves you

[2Co.5:17] Therefore if any man be in Christ, he is a new creature: old things are passed away; behold, all things are become new.
[Phl.3:13] Brothers, I do not consider that I have made it my own. But one thing I do: forgetting what lies behind and straining forward to what lies ahead, (ESV)
[Jer.29:11] For I know the plans I have for you," declares the Lord, "plans to prosper you and not to harm you, plans to give you hope and a future. (NIV)
[Rev.3:9] Behold, I will make those of the synagogue of Satan who say that they are Jews and are not, but lie--behold, I will make them come and bow down before your feet and they will learn that I have loved you.

My beloved child,

Don't be bothered about what others say about you or how they look at you. You are perfect when I made you. [Eze.27:4] Though you may feel that you are not the brightest one in others' eyes, and have always been underestimated, I will lift you up [Job22:29], and will crown you with glory and honor. [Psm.8:5] Focus on me and rest in me.

Heavenly Father who deeply loves you

[Eze.27:4] Your borders are in the middle of the seas, your builders have perfected your beauty.

[Job22:29] When people are brought low and you say, 'Lift them up!' then he will save the downcast. (NIV)

[Psm.8:5] For you have made him a little lower than the angels, and have crowned him with glory and honor.

My beloved child,

Looking at you, my heart is fully satisfied. You have a heart of Christ listening to my voice and understanding my thoughts. Would you feed my lambs for me? [Jhn.21:15] Bravely share what you have learned with people who are in need. Be guided by my Spirit [Jhn.16:13] and share testimony of Jesus, you will experience miracles. [Act.14:3]

Heavenly Father who deeply loves you

[Jhn.21:15] So when they had dined, Jesus said to Simon Peter, Simon, son of Jonas, love you me more than these? He said to him, Yes, Lord; you know that I love you. He said to him, Feed my lambs.

[Jhn.16:13] However, when he, the Spirit of truth, is come, he will guide you into all truth: for he shall not speak of himself; but whatever he shall hear, that shall he speak: and he will show you things to come.

[Act.14:3] Long time therefore stayed they speaking boldly in the Lord, which gave testimony to the word of his grace, and granted signs and wonders to be done by their hands.

My beloved child,

Rejoice in Jesus always. [Phl.4:4] I know the burdens in your life are almost crushing you out. I hear the crying of your heart. Come to me my beloved and I will give you rest. [Mat.11:28] Pray and pass the burdens to me, because I am the LORD who will renew your strength and make you mount up with wings like an eagle. [Isa.40:29-31] Again, rejoice.

Heavenly Father who deeply loves you

[Phl.4:4] Rejoice in the Lord always: and again I say, Rejoice.

[Mat.11:28] Come to me, all you that labor and are heavy laden, and I will give you rest.

[Isa.40:29-31] 29) He gives power to the faint; and to them that have no might he increases strength. **30)** Even the youths shall faint and be weary, and the young men shall utterly fall: **31)** But they that wait on the LORD shall renew their strength; they shall mount up with wings as eagles; they shall run, and not be weary; and they shall walk, and not faint.

My beloved child,

This world is full of lies, and full of robberies. [Nah.3:1] People treat you injustice, and you do not only lose property but are deeply hurt. Come to me my beloved child, I am your comforter. [Isa.51:12] I will restore what you have lost and double your portion. [Isa.61:7] Forgive and pay back the evil with blessing so that you will obtain a blessing. [1Pe.3:9]

Heavenly Father who deeply loves you

[Nah.3:1] Woe to the bloody city! it is all full of lies and robbery; the prey departs not;
[Isa.51:12] I, even I, am he that comforts you: who are you, that you should be afraid of a man that shall die, and of the son of man which shall be made as grass;
[Isa.61:7] Instead of your shame you will receive a double portion, and instead of disgrace you will rejoice in your inheritance. And so you will inherit a double portion in your land, and everlasting joy will be yours. (NIV)
[1Pe.3:9] Do not repay evil for evil or reviling for reviling, but on the contrary, bless, for to this you were called, that you may obtain a blessing. (ESV)

My beloved child,

When you are looking for new opportunities, or when a new chance is opening to you, don't forget to seek Jesus first, because Jesus is who holds the Key of King David, and can open a door of wonderful new way for you, or shut the door of a path that may harm you later. [Rev.3:7] There may be many animosities [1Co.16:9] but no one can close the doors Jesus opened for you.

Heavenly Father who deeply loves you

[Rev.3:7] And to the angel of the church in Philadelphia write; These things said he that is holy, he that is true, he that has the key of David, he that opens, and no man shuts; and shuts, and no man opens;
[1Co.16:9] For a great door and effectual is opened to me, and there are many adversaries.

My beloved child,

Suffering is never the plan I have for you. [Jer.29:11] Come close to me and take the Holy Communion to remember Jesus. By Jesus's injury and his broken body, you are healed and my Shalom Peace is with you. [Isa.53:5]

Heavenly Father who deeply loves you

p.s. Hold on to the faith, but if you are ill, please go to a doctor and don't stop medical treatment before the doctor approves.

[Jer.29:11] For I know the plans I have for you," declares the Lord, "plans to prosper you and not to harm you, plans to give you hope and a future. (NIV)

[Isa.53:5] But he was wounded for our transgressions, he was bruised for our iniquities: the chastisement of our peace was on him; and with his stripes we are healed.

My beloved child,

You are living in grace, not in law. [Rom.5:2]
Don't judge others, [Luk.6:37] because there
may be somethings you don't know or the
truth is not as what you saw. You are the royal
priesthood of my holy nation. Be merciful to
those who you don't like and pray for them,
as I am merciful to you. [1Pe.2:9-10]

Heavenly Father who deeply loves you

[**Rom.5:2**] By whom also we have access by faith into this grace wherein we stand, and rejoice in hope of the glory of God.
[**Luk.6:37**] Judge not, and you shall not be judged: condemn not, and you shall not be condemned: forgive, and you shall be forgiven
[**1Pe.2:9-10**] **9)** But you are a chosen generation, a royal priesthood, an holy nation, a peculiar people; that you should show forth the praises of him who has called you out of darkness into his marvelous light; **10)** Which in time past were not a people, but are now the people of God: which had not obtained mercy, but now have obtained mercy.

My beloved child,

Do not stock up treasures on earth for yourselves, but stock up treasures in heaven. [Mat.6:19-20] I promise that you will receive many times more in this life. [Luk.18:29-30] Yes, in this lifetime! You may live a life on earth as in heaven, [Mat.6:10] only if you live in Jesus, pray to me, and follow my spirit. [Rom.6:11]

Heavenly Father who deeply loves you

[Mat.6:19-20] 19) Lay not up for yourselves treasures on earth, where moth and rust does corrupt, and where thieves break through and steal: **20)** But lay up for yourselves treasures in heaven, where neither moth nor rust does corrupt, and where thieves do not break through nor steal:

[Luk.18:29-30] 29) And he said to them, "Truly, I say to you, there is no one who has left house or wife or brothers or parents or children, for the sake of the kingdom of God, **30)** who will not receive many times more in this time, and in the age to come eternal life." (ESV)

[Mat.6:10] Your kingdom come, Your will be done in earth, as it is in heaven.

[Rom.6:11] so also ye, reckon yourselves to be dead indeed to the sin, and living to God in Jesus Christ our Lord. (YLT)

My beloved child,

Do not doubt. I promise "According to your faith, be it to you"! [Mat.9:29] Do guard your heart, [Pro.4:23] because you will receive what you believe. [Mat.21:22] Remember that you are in Christ and you are righteous. [Rom.3:22] Things will happen through Jesus, [Jhn.1:3] not happen according to what your circumstance is or what others say.

Heavenly Father who deeply loves you

[Mat.9:29] Then touched he their eyes, saying, According to your faith be it to you.
[Rro.4:23] Above all else, guard your heart, for everything you do flows from it. (NIV)
[Mat.21:22] And all things, whatever you shall ask in prayer, believing, you shall receive.
[Rom.3:22] even the righteousness of God through faith in Jesus Christ unto all them that believe; for there is no distinction; (ASV)
[Jhn.1:3] all things through him did happen, and without him happened not even one thing that hath happened. (YLT)

My beloved child,

Do not envy sinners, but always be in awe of me. [Pro.23:17] If you know how the fullness you are in Christ, [Col.2:9-10] you will not be jealous. Pray and ask me, I will grant what you ask for. [Jas.4:2 & Jhn.16:24] Do not envy, because those envy will not inherit the reign of Jesus. [Gal.5:21]

Heavenly Father who deeply loves you

[Pro.23:17] Let not your heart envy sinners: but be you in the fear of the LORD all the day long.

[Col.2:9-10] 9) For in him dwells all the fullness of the Godhead bodily. **10)** And you are complete in him, which is the head of all principality and power:

[Jas.4:2] You desire but do not have, so you kill. You covet but you cannot get what you want, so you quarrel and fight. You do not have because you do not ask God. (NIV)

[Jhn.16:24] Till now have you asked nothing in my name: ask, and you shall receive, that your joy may be full.

[Gal.5:21] envyings, murders, drunkennesses, revellings, and such like, of which I tell you before, as I also said before, that those doing such things the reign of God shall not inherit. (YLT)

My beloved child,

You are wondering how long have to wait?
Rest in me and wait patiently [Psm.37:7],
because there will be your season. [Ecc.3:1]
Your chance is coming. The right person and
right things are coming your way. Have faith
in me, and wait patiently like Abraham
[Heb.6:15], you will soon receive what you are
longing for.

Heavenly Father who deeply loves you

[Psm.37:7] Rest in the LORD, and wait patiently for him: fret not yourself because of him who prospers in his way, because of the man who brings wicked devices to pass.
[Ecc.3:1] For everything there is a season, and a time for every purpose under heaven. (ASV)
[Heb.6:15] And thus Abraham, having patiently waited, obtained the promise. (ESV)

My beloved child,

I know there are many worries in you, about job, about relationship, about future, etc. Don't worry & be happy. [Phl.4:6] Keep smiling and pray to me with thanks. [1Ts.5:16-18] You can wisely find the solutions in my words, and overcome all problems and difficulties. [2Ti.3:15-17] You know that I have prepared all good things for you. [Jos.23:14]

Heavenly Father who deeply loves you

[Phl.4:6] In nothing be anxious; but in everything by prayer and supplication with thanksgiving let your requests be made known unto God. (ASV)

[1Ts.5:16-18] 16) Rejoice always; **17)** pray without ceasing; **18)** in everything give thanks: for this is the will of God in Christ Jesus to you-ward. (ASV)

[2Ti.3:15-17] 15) And that from a child you have known the holy scriptures, which are able to make you wise to salvation through faith which is in Christ Jesus. **16)** All scripture is given by inspiration of God, and is profitable for doctrine, for reproof, for correction, for instruction in righteousness: **17)** That the man of God may be perfect, thoroughly furnished to all good works.

[Jos.23:14] And, behold, this day I am going the way of all the earth: and you know in all your hearts and in all your souls, that not one thing has failed of all the good things which the LORD your God spoke concerning you; all are come to pass to you, and not one thing has failed thereof.

My beloved child,

In this turbulent world, some people or some things make you worry or feel nervous and cannot have a good sleep. You know what? I am watching over you & your family, and keep you & your family from all harm now and forevermore. [Psm.121:7-8] I am your refuge. No damage will happen to you. No disaster will come near your house. [Psm.91:2-11] I will protect you & your family coming and going.

Heavenly Father who deeply loves you

[Psm.121:7-8] 7) The LORD shall preserve you from all evil: he shall preserve your soul. 8) The LORD shall preserve your going out and your coming in from this time forth, and even for ever more.

[Psm.91:2-11] 2) I will say of the LORD, He is my refuge and my fortress: my God; in him will I trust. 3) Surely he shall deliver you from the snare of the fowler, and from the noisome pestilence. 4) He shall cover you with his feathers, and under his wings shall you trust: his truth shall be your shield and buckler. 5) You shall not be afraid for the terror by night; nor for the arrow that flies by day; 6) Nor for the pestilence that walks in darkness; nor for the destruction that wastes at noonday. 7) A thousand shall fall at your side, and ten thousand at your right hand; but it shall not come near you. 8) Only with your eyes shall you behold and see the reward of the wicked. 9) Because you have made the LORD, which is my refuge, even the most High, your habitation; 10) There shall no evil befall you, neither shall any plague come near your dwelling. 11) For he shall give his angels charge over you, to keep you in all your ways.

My beloved child,

You are facing a huge difficulty and find no one is with you or can help you. Do not be afraid, for I am with you. Do not look around, for I am your God [Isa.41:10]. The battle is mine! [1Sa.17:47] I will strengthen you and help you. Just seek me and ask me for help. I am the one who make the heaven and earth. [Psm.121:1-2] There is nothing too hard for me. [Jer.32:17]

Heavenly Father who deeply loves you

[Isa.41:10] Fear you not; for I am with you: be not dismayed; for I am your God: I will strengthen you; yes, I will help you; yes, I will uphold you with the right hand of my righteousness.

[1Sa.17:47] And all this assembly shall know that the LORD saves not with sword and spear: for the battle is the LORD's, and he will give you into our hands.

[Psm.121:1-2] 1) I will lift up my eyes to the hills, from where comes my help. 2) My help comes from the LORD, which made heaven and earth.

[Jer.32:17] Ah Lord GOD! behold, you have made the heaven and the earth by your great power and stretched out arm, and there is nothing too hard for you:

My beloved child,

You have long for something for a long time, a good relationship, good fortune, good health, better job position, good performance of children, etc. You feel frustrated and wonder whether it will come to pass? Do not give up and keep praying, [Luk.18:1] because it will surely come at an appointed time and will not delay. [Hab.2:3]

Heavenly Father who deeply loves you

[Luk.18:1] Then Jesus told his disciples a parable to show them that they should always pray and not give up. (NIV)
[Hab.2:3] For still the vision awaits its appointed time; it hastens to the end--it will not lie. If it seems slow, wait for it; it will surely come; it will not delay. (ESV)

My beloved child,

Though it is other's fault that makes you suffer, do not be angered or bothered by wrongdoers' well-being. [Pro.24:19; Psm.37:6-9] Look at young David who had not wronged to King Saul and what he had done benefiting Saul greatly [1Sa.19:4]; however, Saul intended to kill David. [1Sa.20:33] David is fear of me and not against Saul [1Sa.24:6]; therefore, I reward him with riches and honor and life. [Pro.22:4]

Heavenly Father who deeply loves you

[Pro.24:19] Fret not yourself because of evil men, neither be you envious at the wicked:

[Psm.37:6-9] 6) And he shall bring forth your righteousness as the light, and your judgment as the noonday. 7) Rest in the LORD, and wait patiently for him: fret not yourself because of him who prospers in his way, because of the man who brings wicked devices to pass. 8) Cease from anger, and forsake wrath: fret not yourself in any wise to do evil. 9) For evildoers shall be cut off: but those that wait on the LORD, they shall inherit the earth.

[1Sa.19:4] Jonathan spoke well of David to Saul his father and said to him, "Let not the king do wrong to his servant David; he has not wronged you, and what he has done has benefited you greatly. (NIV)

[1Sa.20:33] But Saul hurled his spear at him to kill him. Then Jonathan knew that his father intended to kill David. (NIV)

[1Sa.24:6] And he said to his men, The LORD forbid that I should do this thing to my master, the LORD's anointed, to stretch forth my hand against him, seeing he is the anointed of the LORD.

[Pro.22:4] The reward for humility and fear of the LORD is riches and honor and life. (ESV)

My beloved child,

I had chosen you before there was the world. [Eph1:4] You are not a fault or an excess. All the beautiful days I have for you are recorded in the book of life. [Psm.139:16] I will give you better things much more than your parents can [Mat.7:11], and grant every perfect gift to you. [Jas.1:17] Because you are the apple of my eye [Deu.32:10], and because you are treasure of mine. [Exo.19:5]

Heavenly Father who deeply loves you

[Eph1:4] According as he has chosen us in him before the foundation of the world, that we should be holy and without blame before him in love:

[Psm.139:16] Your eyes saw my unformed body; all the days ordained for me were written in your book before one of them came to be. (NIV)

[Mat.7:11] If you then, being evil, know how to give good gifts to your children, how much more shall your Father which is in heaven give good things to them that ask him?

[Jas.1:17] Every good gift and every perfect gift is from above, and comes down from the Father of lights, with whom is no ficklenss, neither shadow of turning.

[Deu.32:10] He found him in a desert land, and in the waste howling wilderness; he led him about, he instructed him, he kept him as the apple of his eye.

[Exo.19:5] Now therefore, if you will obey my voice indeed, and keep my covenant, then you shall be a peculiar treasure to me above all people: for all the earth is mine:

My beloved child,

It is good to exercise, and it is also good to take a healthy diet. However, do you know why Moses' eyes were not dim nor his strength gone in his year 120? [Deu34:7] Because Moses saw Jesus on the cross in his spirit eyes. [Heb.11:26-27] Try to see Jesus in the whole bible and remember him in every aspect of your life, and put Jesus in the center of your life. You will be renewed and keep young & healthy like Moses.

Heavenly Father who deeply loves you

[Deu34:7] And Moses was an hundred and twenty years old when he died: his eye was not dim, nor his natural force abated.

[Heb.11:26-27] 26) Esteeming the reproach of Christ greater riches than the treasures in Egypt: for he had respect to the recompense of the reward. **27)** By faith he forsook Egypt, not fearing the wrath of the king: for he endured, as seeing him who is invisible.

My beloved child,

You are deeply hurt by someone you trust most. Your heart is bleeding so you decide to close your heart and don't trust others anymore. My beloved child, I bind up the broken. [Eze34:16] Release your sorrow to me. I will turn your mourning into gladness and give you comfort and joy instead of sorrow. [Jer.31:13] You will experience an unusual blessing. [Gen.12:2]

Heavenly Father who deeply loves you

[Eze34:16] I will seek that which was lost, and bring again that which was driven away, and will bind up that which was broken, and will strengthen that which was sick: but I will destroy the fat and the strong; I will feed them with judgment.

[Jer.31:13] Then young women will dance and be glad, young men and old as well. I will turn their mourning into gladness; I will give them comfort and joy instead of sorrow. (NIV)

[Gen.12:2] And I will make of you a great nation, and I will bless you, and make your name great; and you shall be a blessing:

My beloved child,

You know what? Love is the most powerful weapon! Do love your enemies, do good to them and pray for them. [Mat.5:44] Do not avenge. [Rom.12:19] Just love people like Jesus loves you. [1Jn.4:11] If you did not wrong to others but are persecuted, you will be blessed and your reward will be great. [Mat.5:10]

Heavenly Father who deeply loves you

[Mat.5:44] But I say to you, Love your enemies, bless them that curse you, do good to them that hate you, and pray for them which spitefully use you, and persecute you;
[Rom.12:19] Beloved, never avenge yourselves, but leave it to the wrath of God, for it is written, "Vengeance is mine, I will repay, says the Lord." (ESV)
[1Jn.4:11] Dear friends, since God so loved us, we also ought to love one another. (NIV)
[Mat.5:10] Blessed are they which are persecuted for righteousness' sake: for theirs is the kingdom of heaven.

My beloved child,

Jesus came to serve you not to be served. [Mak.10:45] Don't be troubled and worried about such a number of things in world or service in church. Sit at my feet, and hear my words first. [Luk.10:39-42] I am the vine; you are the branches. Remain in me and you will bear much more fruit. [Jhn.15:5]

Heavenly Father who deeply loves you

[Mak.10:45] For even the Son of man came not to be ministered to, but to minister, and to give his life a ransom for many
[Luk.10:39-42] 39) And she had a sister called Mary, which also sat at Jesus' feet, and heard his word. **40)** But Martha was encumbered about much serving, and came to him, and said, Lord, do you not care that my sister has left me to serve alone? bid her therefore that she help me. **41)** And Jesus answered and said to her, Martha, Martha, you are careful and troubled about many things: **42)** But one thing is needful: and Mary has chosen that good part, which shall not be taken away from her.
[Jhn.15:5] I am the vine, you are the branches: He that stays in me, and I in him, the same brings forth much fruit: for without me you can do nothing.

My beloved child,

Do not depend on your own understanding. [Pro.3:5] Do not put your trust in human beings, who cannot truly help you. [Psm.146:3] Also do not put your hope in wealth. But only depend on me. [1Ti.6:17] Because not by might nor by power, but by my Spirit [Zec.4:6] that accomplishment. Solely trust in me and commit your way to me. I will make it for you. [Psm.37:5]

Heavenly Father who deeply loves you

[Pro.3:5] Trust in the LORD with all your heart; and lean not to your own understanding.

[Psm.146:3] Put not your trust in princes, nor in the son of man, in whom there is no help.

[1Ti.6:17] Command those who are rich in this present world not to be arrogant nor to put their hope in wealth, which is so uncertain, but to put their hope in God, who richly provides us with everything for our enjoyment. (NIV)

[Zec.4:6] Then he answered and spoke to me, saying, This is the word of the LORD to Zerubbabel, saying, Not by might, nor by power, but by my spirit, said the LORD of hosts.

[Psm.37:5] Commit your way to the LORD; trust also in him; and he shall bring it to pass.

My beloved child,

You may feel frustrated about some addictions: A habit or a relationship. I know all your struggles but do you know that you don't need to condemn yourself [Rom.8:1] or fight by yourself? Jesus loves you. Depend on Jesus, your perfect savior, through his love to you, you can overcome all. [Rom.8:37] Rest in Jesus' love, live through him [1Jn.4:9] and you will be renewed. [Tit.3:5]

Heavenly Father who deeply loves you

[Rom.8:1] There is therefore now no condemnation to them which are in Christ Jesus, who walk not after the flesh, but after the Spirit.

[Rom.8:37] No, in all these things we are more than conquerors through him that loved us.

[1Jn.4:9] In this was manifested the love of God toward us, because that God sent his only begotten Son into the world, that we might live through him.

[Tit.3:5] he saved us, not because of works done by us in righteousness, but according to his own mercy, by the washing of regeneration and renewal of the Holy Spirit, (ESV)

My beloved child,

You wonder why this happens? Even people may say it is a punishment. No. Jesus had suffered and borne all punishment for you on the cross so you may have peace & hope in life. [1Pe.2:24] Don't be afraid; only believe. [Mak.5:36] Keep your faith in Jesus and his love for you. Things are too marvelous for you to understand. [Job42:3] My ways are higher than your ways. [Isa.55:9] You will realize someday.

Heavenly Father who deeply loves you

[1Pe.2:24] He himself bore our sins" in his body on the cross, so that we might die to sins and live for righteousness; "by his wounds you have been healed. (NIV)

[Mak.5:36] As soon as Jesus heard the word that was spoken, he said to the ruler of the synagogue, Be not afraid, only believe.

[Job42:3] Who is he that hides counsel without knowledge? therefore have I uttered that I understood not; things too wonderful for me, which I knew not.

[Isa.55:9] For as the heavens are higher than the earth, so are my ways higher than your ways, and my thoughts than your thoughts.

My beloved child,

You are so kind and tender to others. People may not notice it, but I know. I am so happy to see Jesus' love flowing out through you. [Gal.5:22] Pluck up your courage to make friends with others, and wherever you go, I will be with you. [Jos.1:9] You will be in favor with many people like Jesus. [Luk.2:52]

Heavenly Father who deeply loves you

[Gal.5:22] But the fruit of the Spirit is love, joy, peace, long-suffering, gentleness, goodness, faith,

[Jos.1:9] Have not I commanded you? Be strong and of a good courage; be not afraid, neither be you dismayed: for the LORD your God is with you wherever you go.

[Luk.2:52] And Jesus increased in wisdom and stature, and in favor with God and man.

My beloved child,

Bad news is overwhelming. It looks hopeless. But what others said or what you feel is not the truth. I am the one who changes times and seasons; who dethrones kings and crowns others. [Dan.2:21] Pray to me and you can ask me to show you the things that will come about. [Isa.45:11] Call on me and I will answer. [Psm.91:15]

Heavenly Father who deeply loves you

[Dan.2:21] And he changes the times and the seasons: he removes kings, and sets up kings: he gives wisdom to the wise, and knowledge to them that know understanding:

[Isa.45:11] Thus said the LORD, the Holy One of Israel, and his Maker, Ask me of things to come concerning my sons, and concerning the work of my hands command you me.

[Psm.91:15] He shall call on me, and I will answer him: I will be with him in trouble; I will deliver him, and honor him.

My beloved child,

Marriage should be honored in all cases.
[Heb.13:4] What God joins together, let no
one separate. [Mak.10:9] Do not abandon the
love you had at first. [Rev.2:4] Love can cover
all wrongs. [Pro.10:12] I can turn your
marriage like the water into best wine.
[Jhn.2:9] And you will experience love more
pleasant than wine. [Son.1:2]

Heavenly Father who deeply loves you

[Heb.13:4] Marriage is honorable in all, and the bed undefiled: but fornicators and adulterers God will judge.

[Mak.10:9] Therefore what God has joined together, let no one separate. (NIV)

[Rev.2:4] But I have this against you, that you have abandoned the love you had at first. (ESV)

[Pro.10:12] Hatred stirs up conflict, but love covers over all wrongs. (NIV)

[Jhn.2:9] and the master of the banquet tasted the water that had been turned into wine. He did not realize where it had come from, though the servants who had drawn the water knew. Then he called the bridegroom aside (NIV)

[Son.1:2] Let him kiss me with the kisses of his mouth: for your love is better than wine.

My beloved child,

Children are a heritage from me. [Psm.127:3]
If you look for a new born baby, pray together
to me and I will grant your entreaty.
[Gen.25:21] I promise my chosen people that
none of you will be childless. [Deu.7:14] My
words will come to pass in their season.
[Luk.1:20] Be patient & do what you have to
do, and you will receive the promise.
[Heb.10:36]

Heavenly Father who deeply loves you

[Psm.127:3] See, children are an heritage of the LORD: and the fruit of the womb is his reward.

[Gen.25:21] And Isaac entreated the LORD for his wife, because she was barren: and the LORD was entreated of him, and Rebekah his wife conceived.

[Deu.7:14] You will be blessed more than any other people; none of your men or women will be childless, nor will any of your livestock be without young. (NIV)

[Luk.1:20] And, behold, you shall be dumb, and not able to speak, until the day that these things shall be performed, because you believe not my words, which shall be fulfilled in their season.

[Heb.10:36] For ye have need of patience, that, having done the will of God, ye may receive the promise. (ASV)

My beloved child,

I know you feel totally hopeless about the situation. Like the dead end of your world. Do you remember that Jesus made people resurrection from death? Jairus' daughter [Luk.8:53-55], widow's son in Nain [Luk.7:14-15], and Lazarus [Jhn.11:43-44]. I am the resurrection and the life. [Jhn.11:25] Keep faith in me and rely on me who raise the dead. [2Co.1:9]

Heavenly Father who deeply loves you

[Luk.8:53-55] 53) And they laughed him to scorn, knowing that she was dead. 54) But he, taking her by the hand, called, saying, Maiden, arise. 55) And her spirit returned, and she rose up immediately: and he commanded that something be given her to eat. (ASV)
[Luk.7:14-15] 14) And he came nigh and touched the bier: and the bearers stood still. And he said, Young man, I say unto thee, Arise. 15) And he that was dead sat up, and began to speak. And he gave him to his mother. (ASV)
[Jhn.11:43-44] 43) And when he thus had spoken, he cried with a loud voice, Lazarus, come forth. 44) And he that was dead came forth, bound hand and foot with grave clothes: and his face was bound about with a napkin. Jesus said to them, Loose him, and let him go.
[Jhn.11:25] Jesus said to her, I am the resurrection, and the life: he that believes in me, though he were dead, yet shall he live:
[2Co.1:9] Indeed, we felt that we had received the sentence of death. But that was to make us rely not on ourselves but on God who raises the dead. (ESV)

My beloved child,

Both wealth and honor come from me.
[1Ch.29:12] However, if one owns everything
desiring, but cannot enjoy it, all are in vain.
[Ecc.6:2] Be humble yourself in front of Jesus,
you will be rich and honored. [Pro.22:4] And
then you can enjoy what in life. [Ecc.8:15]
Because Jesus came that you may have life
and have more abundantly. [Jhn.10:10]

Heavenly Father who deeply loves you

[1Ch.29:12] Both riches and honor come of you, and you reign over all; and in your hand is power and might; and in your hand it is to make great, and to give strength to all.
[Ecc.6:2] A man to whom God has given riches, wealth, and honor, so that he wants nothing for his soul of all that he desires, yet God gives him not power to eat thereof, but a stranger eats it: this is vanity, and it is an evil disease.
[Pro.22:4] By humility and the fear of the LORD are riches, and honor, and life.
[Ecc.8:15] Then I commended mirth, because a man has no better thing under the sun, than to eat, and to drink, and to be merry: for that shall abide with him of his labor the days of his life, which God gives him under the sun.
[Jhn.10:10] The thief comes not, but for to steal, and to kill, and to destroy: I am come that they might have life, and that they might have it more abundantly.

My beloved child,

Do not put your faith in every spirit, but test whether it is from God. [1Jn.4:1-3] Also beware of false prophets, they look like good sheep but are cruel wolves inside. [Mat.7:15] If you don't know how to distinguish between right and wrong [1Ki3:9], just ask me for wisdom, and I will give it to you. [Jas.1:5]

Heavenly Father who deeply loves you

[1Jn.4:1-3] 1) Beloved, believe not every spirit, but try the spirits whether they are of God: because many false prophets are gone out into the world. **2)** Hereby know you the Spirit of God: Every spirit that confesses that Jesus Christ is come in the flesh is of God: **3)** And every spirit that confesses not that Jesus Christ is come in the flesh is not of God: and this is that spirit of antichrist, whereof you have heard that it should come; and even now already is it in the world.

[Mat.7:15] Beware of false prophets, which come to you in sheep's clothing, but inwardly they are ravening wolves.

[1Ki3:9] Give therefore your servant an understanding heart to judge your people, that I may discern between good and bad: for who is able to judge this your so great a people?

[Jas.1:5] and if any of you do lack wisdom, let him ask from God, who is giving to all liberally, and not reproaching, and it shall be given to him; (YLT)

My beloved child,

My words of grace can build you up to get the inheritance [Act.20:32] which is inherited in Jesus Christ by the promise to Abraham. [Gal.3:29] The Holy Spirit in you is the guarantee of the inheritance. [Eph.1:13-14] Pray to open the eyes of your heart and you will know the riches of his glorious inheritance in you. [Eph.1:18]

Heavenly Father who deeply loves you

[Act.20:32] And now, brothers, I commend you to God, and to the word of his grace, which is able to build you up, and to give you an inheritance among all them which are sanctified.

[Gal.3:29] And if you be Christ's, then are you Abraham's seed, and heirs according to the promise.

[Eph.1:13-14] 13) In him you also, when you heard the word of truth, the gospel of your salvation, and believed in him, were sealed with the promised Holy Spirit, **14)** who is the guarantee of our inheritance until we acquire possession of it, to the praise of his glory. (ESV)

[Eph.1:18] The eyes of your understanding being enlightened; that you may know what is the hope of his calling, and what the riches of the glory of his inheritance in the saints,

My beloved child,

The redemption grace is through Jesus Christ
to you. [Eph.1:7-8] Not because of anything
people have done. [2Ti.1:9] Therefore, it
cannot be based on good works [Rom.11:6].
Those who were trying to be justified by their
own good behaviors were fallen away from
grace, [Gal.5:4] which they had already
received from Jesus Christ. [Jhn.1:16-17]

Heavenly Father who deeply loves you

[Eph.1:7-8] 7) In whom we have redemption through his blood, the forgiveness of sins, according to the riches of his grace; **8)** Wherein he has abounded toward us in all wisdom and prudence;

[2Ti.1:9] Who has saved us, and called us with an holy calling, not according to our works, but according to his own purpose and grace, which was given us in Christ Jesus before the world began,

[Rom.11:6] And if by grace, then it cannot be based on works; if it were, grace would no longer be grace. (NIV)

[Gal.5:4] You who are trying to be justified by the law have been alienated from Christ; you have fallen away from grace. (NIV)

[Jhn.1:16-17] 16) Out of his fullness we have all received grace in place of grace already given. **17)** For the law was given through Moses; grace and truth came through Jesus Christ. (NIV)

My beloved child,

Remember that all your mistakes, fault, or sins are forgiven, because you are in Jesus [Col.1:13-14] and you are righteous. [Rom.3:24] In Jesus' grace, no sinful nature can overtake you. [Rom.6:14] Your future will get better and better. [Rro.4:18] Surely I bless you and surround you with favor as with a shield. [Psm.5:12]

Heavenly Father who deeply loves you

[Col.1:13-14] 13) Who has delivered us from the power of darkness, and has translated us into the kingdom of his dear Son: 14) In whom we have redemption through his blood, even the forgiveness of sins:

[Rom.3:24] being declared righteous freely by His grace through the redemption that [is] in Christ Jesus, (YLT)

[Rom.6:14] For sin shall not have dominion over you: for you are not under the law, but under grace.

[Rro.4:18] But the path of the righteous is as the dawning light, That shineth more and more unto the perfect day. (ASV)

[Psm.5:12] Surely, Lord, you bless the righteous; you surround them with your favor as with a shield. (NIV)

My beloved child,

Cross is not just a symbol, or a decoration. The moment my beloved son, Jesus, said "It is finished" on the cross. [Jhn.19:30] The salvation work on all human beings had done. He bears all curses on you so you may receive all blessings. [Gal.3:13-14] Because of his redemption, you are able to be my child & with me, [Jhn.14:6] to enjoy all good things that I prepared for you. [Rom.8:32] This is my love for you. [Rom.5:8]

Heavenly Father who deeply loves you

[Jhn.19:30] When Jesus therefore had received the vinegar, he said, It is finished: and he bowed his head, and gave up his spirit. (ASV)

[Gal.3:13-14] 13) Christ has redeemed us from the curse of the law, being made a curse for us: for it is written, Cursed is every one that hangs on a tree: 14) That the blessing of Abraham might come on the Gentiles through Jesus Christ; that we might receive the promise of the Spirit through faith.

[Jhn.14:6] Jesus said to him, I am the way, the truth, and the life: no man comes to the Father, but by me.

[Rom.8:32] He who did not spare his own Son but gave him up for us all, how will he not also with him graciously give us all things? (ESV)

[Rom.5:8] but God shows his love for us in that while we were still sinners, Christ died for us. (ESV)

My beloved child,

I know the sorrow in your heart. Let me wipe away all tears from your eyes [Isa.25:8], and be your comforter. [2Ts.2:16-17] I am the Lord who will turn your wailing into dancing, and remove your sackcloth and cloth you with joy. [Psm.30:11] The grace you are in is the best reason that you may always rejoice. [Rom.5:2]

Heavenly Father who deeply loves you

[Isa.25:8] he will swallow up death forever. The Sovereign Lord will wipe away the tears from all faces; he will remove his people's disgrace from all the earth. The Lord has spoken. (NIV)

[2Ts.2:16-17] 16) Now our Lord Jesus Christ himself, and God our Father who loved us and gave us eternal comfort and good hope through grace, **17)** comfort your hearts and establish them in every good work and word. (ASV)

[Psm.30:11] You turned my wailing into dancing; you removed my sackcloth and clothed me with joy, (NIV)

[Rom.5:2] By whom also we have access by faith into this grace wherein we stand, and rejoice in hope of the glory of God.

My beloved child,

I know you are diligent and eager to build wealth. However, do not rush for money. [Pro.28:22] Just read my words and ask me for wisdom, this is the way for enduring wealth. [Pro.8:18] My blessing makes you rich without sorrow. [Pro.10:22] Seek me and see me as your treasure first [Job22:25], and what you decide on will be done. [Job22:28]

Heavenly Father who deeply loves you

[Pro.28:22] He that hastens to be rich has an evil eye, and considers not that poverty shall come on him.

[Pro.8:18] Riches and honor are with me, enduring wealth and righteousness. (ESV)

[Pro.10:22] The blessing of the LORD makes rich, and he adds no sorrow with it. (ESV)

[Job22:25] And the Almighty will be thy treasure, And precious silver unto thee. (ASV)

[Job22:28] What you decide on will be done, and light will shine on your ways. (NIV)

My beloved child,

True love is selfless. [1Co.13:5] If we give all we have to the poor and suffer for others, but not out of love, all are in vain. [1Co.13:3] But you don't need to feel frustrated, because I first love you. [1Jh.4:19] By the Holy Spirit, you may be full of love, [Rom.5:5] and be able to love others, [1Ts.3:12] and love your spouse like Christ loved the Church. [Eph.5:25]

Heavenly Father who deeply loves you

[1Co.13:5] Does not behave itself unseemly, seeks not her own, is not easily provoked, thinks no evil;
[1Co.13:3] If I give all I possess to the poor and give over my body to hardship that I may boast, but do not have love, I gain nothing. (NIV)
[1Jh.4:19] We love, because he first loved us. (ASV)
[Rom.5:5] and the hope doth not make ashamed, because the love of God hath been poured forth in our hearts through the Holy Spirit that hath been given to us. (YLT)
[1Ts.3:12] and may the Lord make you increase and abound in love for one another and for all, as we do for you, (ESV)
[Eph.5:25] Husbands, love your wives, even as Christ also loved the church, and gave himself up for it; (ASV)

My beloved child,

I am pleased to have all fullness dwell in Jesus
[Col.1:19]; therefore, anyone who is in Jesus
[1Co.3:23], all things are this person's.
[1Co.3:21] Be abide in Jesus and let my words
abide in you, and anything you ask for will be
done for you. [Jhn.15:7] No matter it is good
health, abundant wealth, happy marriage and
family, good reputation and honor, or even
innovative ability, all will be fulfilled in you.
[Psm.20:4]

Heavenly Father who deeply loves you

[Col.1:19] For God was pleased to have all his fullness dwell in him, (NIV)

[1Co.3:23] And you are Christ's; and Christ is God's.

[1Co.3:21] Wherefore let no one glory in men. For all things are yours (ASV)

[Jhn.15:7] If you abide in me, and my words abide in you, ask whatever you wish, and it will be done for you. (ESV)

[Psm.20:4] May he grant you your heart's desire and fulfill all your plans! (ESV)

My beloved child,

Take actions by faith. [2Co.5:7] Don't be afraid. I am with you. [2Sa.7:9] Listen to the Holy Spirit and you will know how to take actions. [Jhn.14:26] Work with me, [1Co.3:9] like the priests who did not dare to step into the Jordan River [Jos.3:13], and you will see the door opened for you like the dry ground showed up in the middle of Jordan River for Israelites to pass over. [Jos.3:17]

Heavenly Father who deeply loves you

[2Co.5:7] For we walk by faith, not by sight:

[2Sa.7:9] And I have been with you wherever you went and have cut off all your enemies from before you. And I will make for you a great name, like the name of the great ones of the earth. (ESV)

[Jhn.14:26] and the Comforter, the Holy Spirit, whom the Father will send in my name, he will teach you all things, and remind you of all things that I said to you. (YLT)

[1Co.3:9] For we are laborers together with God: you are God's husbandry, you are God's building.

[Jos.3:13] And it shall come to pass, as soon as the soles of the feet of the priests that bear the ark of the LORD, the LORD of all the earth, shall rest in the waters of Jordan, that the waters of Jordan shall be cut off from the waters that come down from above; and they shall stand on an heap.

[Jos.3:17] And the priests that bore the ark of the covenant of the LORD stood firm on dry ground in the middle of Jordan, and all the Israelites passed over on dry ground, until all the people were passed clean over Jordan.

My beloved child,

Yes, I'm more than willing to heal you. [Mat.8:2-3] Don't condemn yourself because I do not condemn you. [Jhn.8:11] You are already forgiven. [Mak.2:5] So forgive others as I forgave you. [Eph.4:32] Do praise in your heart [Psm.103:2], because all your iniquities are forgiven and all your diseases are healed. [Psm.103:3]

Heavenly Father who deeply loves you

[Mat.8:2-3] **2)** And, behold, there came a leper and worshipped him, saying, Lord, if you will, you can make me clean. **3)** And Jesus put forth his hand, and touched him, saying, I will; be you clean. And immediately his leprosy was cleansed.

[Jhn.8:11] She said, No man, Lord. And Jesus said to her, Neither do I condemn you: go, and sin no more.

[Mak.2:5] And Jesus seeing their faith saith unto the sick of the palsy, Son, thy sins are forgiven. (ASV)

[Eph.4:32] And be you kind one to another, tenderhearted, forgiving one another, even as God for Christ's sake has forgiven you.

[Psm.103:2] Praise the Lord, my soul, and forget not all his benefits (NIV)

[Psm.103:3] Who forgives all your iniquities; who heals all your diseases;

My beloved child,

I have many names among human beings.
Jehovah-Jireh [Gen.22:14], Jehovah-Nissi
[Exo.17:15], Jehovah-Shalom [Jug.6:24], and
many others. However, your "Father" is the
name I enjoy most. [Isa.63:16] Though earthly
father or mother may forsake you [Psm.27:10],
my love to you endures forever. [Psm.138:8] I
am so happy that I may find you back in my
arms. [Luk.15:20 & Luk.15:32]

 Heavenly Father who deeply loves you

[Gen.22:14] and Abraham calleth the name of
that place `Jehovah-Jireh,' because it is said
this day in the mount, `Jehovah doth provide.'
(YLT)

[**Exo.17:15**] And Moses built an altar, and called the name of it Jehovah-nissi; (ASV)

[**Jug.6:24**] Then Gideon built an altar there to the LORD, and called it Jehovahshalom: to this day it is yet in Ophrah of the Abiezrites.

[**Isa.63:16**] Doubtless you are our father, though Abraham be ignorant of us, and Israel acknowledge us not: you, O LORD, are our father, our redeemer; your name is from everlasting.

[**Psm.27:10**] When my father and my mother forsake me, then the LORD will take me up.

[**Psm.138:8**] The Lord will vindicate me; your love, Lord, endures forever— do not abandon the works of your hands. (NIV)

[**Luk.15:20**] So he got up and went to his father. "But while he was still a long way off, his father saw him and was filled with compassion for him; he ran to his son, threw his arms around him and kissed him. (NIV)

[**Luk.15:32**] But it was meet to make merry and be glad: for this thy brother was dead, and is alive again; and was lost, and is found. (ASV)

My beloved child,

You are always with me, and all that I have is yours. [Luk.15:31] I bless my children to a degree that you may have great amount left over. [2Ch.31:10] However, my heart is also with helpless people. [Deu.10:18] Would you help them and share what you have with them? [Deu.14:29] So I may bless you more, because give and it should be given to you. [Luk.6:38]

Heavenly Father who deeply loves you

[Luk.15:31] And he said to him, Son, you are ever with me, and all that I have is yours.

[2Ch.31:10] And Azariah the chief priest of the house of Zadok answered him, and said, Since the people began to bring the offerings into the house of the LORD, we have had enough to eat, and have left plenty: for the LORD has blessed his people; and that which is left is this great store.

[Deu.10:18] He defends the cause of the fatherless and the widow, and loves the foreigner residing among you, giving them food and clothing. (NIV)

[Deu.14:29] And the Levite, (because he has no part nor inheritance with you,) and the stranger, and the fatherless, and the widow, which are within your gates, shall come, and shall eat and be satisfied; that the LORD your God may bless you in all the work of your hand which you do.

[Luk.6:38] `Give, and it shall be given to you; good measure, pressed, and shaken, and running over, they shall give into your bosom; for with that measure with which ye measure, it shall be measured to you again.' (YLT)

My beloved child,

Grace, unmerited favor, is Jesus, who himself
has paid the price at the cross for all who
believe in him. [Heb.10:10] Therefore, by faith
[Rom.5:2] you may have eternal life [Jhn.3:15],
and enjoy all the blessings from me. [Deu.28:2]
You surely can have confidence that you are
my greatly blessed [Heb.6:14], highly favored
[Psm.30:5] and deeply loved child [Jhn3:16].

Heavenly Father who deeply loves you

[Heb.10:10] By which will we have been sanctified through the offering of the body of Jesus Christ once for all. (ASV)
[Rom.5:2] By whom also we have access by faith into this grace wherein we stand, and rejoice in hope of the glory of God.
[Jhn.3:15] That whoever believes in him should not perish, but have eternal life.
[Deu.28:2] And all these blessings shall come on you, and overtake you, if you shall listen to the voice of the LORD your God.
[Heb.6:14] Saying, Surely blessing I will bless you, and multiplying I will multiply you.
[Psm.30:5] For his anger is but for a moment; His favor is for a life-time: Weeping may tarry for the night, But joy cometh in the morning. (ASV)
[Jhn3:16] For God so loved the world, that he gave his only begotten Son, that whosoever believeth on him should not perish, but have eternal life. (ASV)

My beloved child,

Submission to my appointed leadership will release my blessing into your life, because I established these authorities. [Rom.13:1] Everyone knows the history that young David killed Goliath. [1Sam.17:51] In the begging, David didn't know it's the moment I set up to bless him [1Sam.17:29], but just obey his father's commend. [1Sam.17:20] So, do submit yourself to the human ordinances. [1Pe.2:13]

Heavenly Father who deeply loves you

[**Rom.13:1**] Let every soul to the higher authorities be subject, for there is no authority except from God, and the authorities existing are appointed by God, (YLT)

[**1Sam.17:51**] Therefore David ran, and stood on the Philistine, and took his sword, and drew it out of the sheath thereof, and slew him, and cut off his head therewith. And when the Philistines saw their champion was dead, they fled.

[**1Sam.17:29**] And David said, What have I now done? Is there not a cause?

[**1Sam.17:20**] And David rose up early in the morning, and left the sheep with a keeper, and took, and went, as Jesse had commanded him; and he came to the trench, as the host was going forth to the fight, and shouted for the battle.

[**1Pe.2:13**] Submit yourselves to every ordinance of man for the Lord's sake: whether it be to the king, as supreme;

My beloved child,

Be faithful in small things [Luk.12:26], and faithful in other's things [Luk.16:12]. Whoever can be trusted with very little can also be trusted with much. [Luk.16:10] If you have been reliable in a very little, then you will be granted the authority for greater. [Luk.19:17] I even choose the base things [1Co.1:28] so do not despise the small thing. [Zec.4:10]

Heavenly Father who deeply loves you

[Luk.12:26] If you then be not able to do that thing which is least, why take you thought for the rest?

[Luk.16:12] And if you have not been faithful in that which is another man's, who shall give you that which is your own?

[Luk.16:10] Whoever can be trusted with very little can also be trusted with much, and whoever is dishonest with very little will also be dishonest with much. (NIV)

[Luk.19:17] And he said to him, Well, you good servant: because you have been faithful in a very little, have you authority over ten cities.

[1Co.1:28] And base things of the world, and things which are despised, has God chosen, yes, and things which are not, to bring to nothing things that are

[Zec.4:10] Who dares despise the day of small things, since the seven eyes of the Lord that range throughout the earth will rejoice when they see the chosen capstone in the hand of Zerubbabel? (NIV)

My beloved child,

You feel the tremendous event happened recently in your life like the oceans rise and thunder roars. Your world is shaken like an earthquake. Be still, and know that I am God. [Psm.46:10] I laid the foundations of the earth with my mighty power. [Job.38:4] I am your refuge and your help. [Psm.46:1] I can do all things [Job.42:2], and my love for you endures forever. [Jer.33:11]

    Heavenly Father who deeply loves you

[Psm.46:10] Be still, and know that I am God: I will be exalted among the heathen, I will be exalted in the earth.

[Job.38:4] Where were you when I laid the foundations of the earth? declare, if you have understanding.

[Psm.46:1] God is our refuge and strength, a very present help in trouble.

[Job.42:2] I know that you can do every thing, and that no thought can be withheld from you.

[Jer.33:11] the voice of mirth and the voice of gladness, the voice of the bridegroom and the voice of the bride, the voices of those who sing, as they bring thank offerings to the house of the LORD: "'Give thanks to the LORD of hosts, for the LORD is good, for his steadfast love endures forever! 'For I will restore the fortunes of the land as at first, says the LORD. (ESV)

My beloved child,

Do you know why King David was victorious in every fight? [2Sa8:6,14] Yes. I made him success, and he is the man after my own heart. [1Sa.13:14] But here is a secret: David is a person always worships and praises to me [1Ch.16:8-9] in Spirit and truth [Jhn.4:24], no matter his circumstance [Psm.35:28], or how people look at him [2Sa:6:16]. This brings my presence, which is the guarantee for the victory. [1Sa.17:47]

Heavenly Father who deeply loves you

[2Sa8:6,14] 6) Then David put garrisons in Aram of Damascus, and the Syrians became servants to David and brought tribute. And the LORD gave victory to David wherever he went. **14)** Then he put garrisons in Edom; throughout all Edom he put garrisons, and all the Edomites became David's servants. And the LORD gave victory to David wherever he went. (ESV)

[1Sa.13:14] But now your kingdom shall not continue: the LORD has sought him a man after his own heart, and the LORD has commanded him to be captain over his people, because you have not kept that which the LORD commanded you.

[1Ch.16:8-9] **8)** Give thanks to the LORD, call on his name, make known his deeds among the people. **9)** Sing to him, sing psalms to him, talk you of all his wondrous works.

[Jhn.4:24] God is a Spirit: and they that worship him must worship in spirit and truth. (ASV)

[Psm.35:28] And my tongue shall speak of your righteousness and of your praise all the day long.

[2Sa:6:16] And as the ark of the LORD came into the city of David, Michal Saul's daughter looked through a window, and saw king David leaping and dancing before the LORD; and she despised him in her heart.

[1Sa.17:47] And all this assembly shall know that the LORD saves not with sword and spear: for the battle is the LORD's, and he will give you into our hands.

My beloved child,

When things don't go your way, like I rejected David to build the temple for me [1Ki.8:19], or when your deepest desire is crumbled into nothing, like Mary's Lazarus was dead, [Jhn.11:14] will you still trust in me? [Job.13:15] I know it is difficult, but you can depend on the faith of Jesus Christ [Gal.3:22] not on your own [Heb.12:2], and depend on Jesus' love to you, and then you can conquer all. [Rom.8:37]

Heavenly Father who deeply loves you

[**1Ki.8:19**] Nevertheless you shall not build the house; but your son that shall come forth out of your loins, he shall build the house to my name.
[**Jhn.11:14**] Then Jesus therefore said unto them plainly, Lazarus is dead. (ASV)
[**Job.13:15**] Though he slay me, yet will I trust in him: but I will maintain my own ways before him.
[**Gal.3:22**] But the scripture has concluded all under sin, that the promise by faith of Jesus Christ might be given to them that believe.
[**Heb.12:2**] looking unto Jesus the author and perfecter of our faith, who for the joy that was set before him endured the cross, despising shame, and hath sat down at the right hand of the throne of God. (ASV)
[**Rom.8:37**] No, in all these things we are more than conquerors through him that loved us.

My beloved child,

The promised land is flowing with milk and honey [Deu.11:9], full of good things that are not brought out by your effort [Deu.6:11], but all the work was finished in the beginning of the world. [Heb.4:3] Therefore, believe in the grace of Jesus [Heb.4:2], and cease your own works. [Heb.4:10] Just wholly follow me like Caleb and Joshua [Num.32:11-12], and you will enjoy the life on earth as in heaven. [Deu.11:21]

   Heavenly Father who deeply loves you

[Deu.11:9] And that you may prolong your days in the land, which the LORD swore to your fathers to give to them and to their seed, a land that flows with milk and honey. [Deu.6:11] And houses full of all good things, which you filled not, and wells dig, which you digged not, vineyards and olive trees, which you planted not; when you shall have eaten and be full;

[Heb.4:3] For we which have believed do enter into rest, as he said, As I have sworn in my wrath, if they shall enter into my rest: although the works were finished from the foundation of the world.

[Heb.4:2] For to us was the gospel preached, as well as to them: but the word preached did not profit them, not being mixed with faith in them that heard it.

[Heb.4:10] For he that is entered into his rest, he also has ceased from his own works, as God did from his.

[Num.32:11-12] 11) Surely none of the men that came up out of Egypt, from twenty years old and upward, shall see the land which I swore to Abraham, to Isaac, and to Jacob; because they have not wholly followed me: 12) Save Caleb the son of Jephunneh the Kenezite, and Joshua the son of Nun: for they have wholly followed the LORD.

[Deu.11:21] That your days may be multiplied, and the days of your children, in the land which the LORD swore to your fathers to give them, as the days of heaven on the earth.

My beloved child,

You have a loving heart toward others, and you are sorrowful for the suffering of people in this vicious era. [2Ti.3:1] Wiping away the tears & being strong, because you are greatly beloved [Dan.10:19] and so precious in my sight [Isa.43:4]. What I'm doing you may not understand now, but later you will realize. [Jhn.13:7] Keep in my love and let me be your comforter. [Jud.1:21]

Heavenly Father who deeply loves you

[2Ti.3:1] This know also, that in the last days perilous times shall come.

[Dan.10:19] And said, O man greatly beloved, fear not: peace be to you, be strong, yes, be strong. And when he had spoken to me, I was strengthened, and said, Let my lord speak; for you have strengthened me.

[Isa.43:4] Since you were precious in my sight, you have been honorable, and I have loved you: therefore will I give men for you, and people for your life.

[Jhn.13:7] Jesus answered and said to him, What I do you know not now; but you shall know hereafter.

[Jud.1:21] Keep yourselves in the love of God, looking for the mercy of our Lord Jesus Christ to eternal life.

My beloved child,

You have been looking for a breakthrough for a long time. I am the way maker and I will guide you. [Mic.2:13] Submit yourself to me [Heb.12:9], and you will see my love & provision like Abraham saw on the mountain in Moriah [Gen.22:12-13]. Praise unto me like Paul and Silas in the prison did, and all the doors will be opened for you. [Act.16:25-26]

Heavenly Father who deeply loves you

[Mic.2:13] The breaker is come up before them: they have broken up, and have passed through the gate, and are gone out by it: and their king shall pass before them, and the LORD on the head of them.

[Heb.12:9] Moreover, we have all had human fathers who disciplined us and we respected them for it. How much more should we submit to the Father of spirits and live! (NIV)

[Gen.22:12-13] 12) He said, "Do not lay your hand on the boy or do anything to him, for now I know that you fear God, seeing you have not withheld your son, your only son, from me." **13)** And Abraham lifted up his eyes and looked, and behold, behind him was a ram, caught in a thicket by his horns. And Abraham went and took the ram and offered it up as a burnt offering instead of his son. (ESV)

[Act.16:25-26] 25) And at midnight Paul and Silas prayed, and sang praises to God: and the prisoners heard them. **26)** And suddenly there was a great earthquake, so that the foundations of the prison were shaken: and immediately all the doors were opened, and every one's bands were loosed.

[Abbreviations] Bible Book List
OLD TESTAMENT

[Gen.] Genesis	[Eze.] Ezekiel
[Exo.] Exodus	[Dan.] Daniel
[Lev.] Leviticus	[Hos.] Hosea
[Num.] Numbers	[Joe.] Joel
[Deu.] Deuteronomy	[Amo.] Amos
[Jos.] Joshua	[Oba.] Obadiah
[Jug.] Judges	[Jon.] Jonah
[Rut.] Ruth	[Mic.] Micah
[1Sa.] 1 Samuel	[Nah.] Nahum
[2Sa.] 2 Samuel	[Hab.] Habakkuk
[1Ki.] 1Kings	[Zep.] Zephaniah
[2Ki.] 2Kings	[Hag.] Haggai
[1Ch.] 1 Chronicles	[Zec.] Zechariah
[2Ch.] 2 Chronicles	[Mal.] Malachi
[Ezr.] Ezra	
[Neh.] Nehemiah	
[Est.] Esther	
[Job] Job	
[Psm.] Psalms	
[Pro.] Proverbs	
[Ecc.] Ecclesiastes	
[Son.] Song of Songs	
[Isa.] Isaiah	
[Jer.] Jeremiah	
[Lam.]Lamentations	

[Abbreviations] Bible Book List
NEW TESTAMENT

[Mat.] Matthew	[Jud.] Jude
[Mak.] Mark	[Rev.] Revelation
[Luk.] Luke	
[Jhn.] John	
[Act.] Acts	
[Rom.] Romans	
[1Co.] 1 Corinthians	
[2Co.] 2 Corinthians	
[Gal.] Galatians	
[Eph.] Ephesians	
[Phl.] Philippians	
[Col.] Colossians	
[1Ts.]1Thessalonians	
[2Ts.]2Thessalonians	
[1Ti.] 1 Timothy	
[2Ti.] 2 Timothy	
[Tit.] Titus	
[Phm.] Philemon	
[Heb.] Hebrews	
[Jas.] James	
[1Pe.] 1 Peter	
[2Pe.] 2 Peter	
[1Jn.] 1 John	
[2Jn.] 2 John	
[3Jn.] 3 John	

Salvation Prayer

If you have never received Jesus as your Savior but you want to invite Jesus into your life as your personal Savior and experience miracles in life, please pray this prayer:

Dear Jesus,

Thank you for loving me and dying for me on the cross. Your precious blood washes away all my sins. I am totally forgiven by your finished work on the cross, and from now on, I'm a beloved child of God. I praise that your resurrection from death is the assurance for my victory in this life and my crown in eternal life. Thank you Jesus, please come into my heart and be my Lord. Amen.

Welcome Home of Heavenly Father! After this prayer, you are a child of God. Please join a bible based church near your home, and start your wonderful new life with Jesus.